Prayers to Find a Godly Spouse

DORIS & DANIEL C. OKPARA

Meditations, Prophetic Declarations and Biblical Foundation for Finding a Life Partner

---

Published By:

Better Life Media.

BETTER LIFE WORLD OUTREACH CENTER.

Website: www.BetterLifeWorld.org

Email: info@betterlifeworld.org

This title and others are available for quantity discounts for sale promotions, gifts, and evangelism. Visit our website or email us to get started.

Any scripture quotation in this book is taken from the King James Version or New International Version, except where stated. Used by permission.

All texts, calls, letters, testimonies, and inquiries are welcome.

CONTENTS

FREE BONUS ...

Download These 4 Powerful Books Today for
FREE... And Take Your Relationship With God
to a New Level.

Go Here to Download:

www.betterlifeworld.org/grow

Dedication

To the Holy Spirit, our present help at all times.

To Chief Gibson & Lolor Rita Anugwom, for an exemplary marriage

To our children, Isaac and Annabel, for teaching us patience.

To you, reading this book; may your prayers be answered and may you have complete joy in your marriage, in Jesus name.

Opening Prayer

"Heavenly Father,

I thank Thee for the institution of marriage. I acknowledge that marriage is Your making and not that of man. As I seek You henceforth for guidance and direction towards a life partner, I am convinced that You will make way for me.

Father, In the Name of Jesus Christ, I ask for Your will to be done in my life as I seek a life partner.

Your Word says in Psalm 37:4 that if I delight myself in THEE – that You will give me the desires of my heart.

LORD, I ask for a godly life partner so that our lives will be lived in your service, forever and ever. Please provide me a partner who will love You and follow after You all the days of their life.

Give me a partner who will love me and take me for who You have made me to be, as I continually grow in THY LOVE.

In Jesus name, I pray."

Introduction

"Those that go searching for love, only manifest their own lovelessness. And the loveless never find love, only the loving find love. And they never have to seek for it." - D. H. LAWRENCE

This book is a collection of notes and discussions shared in singles' meetings that we've been privileged to lead. I believe that these truths will help any person seeking a life partner – man or woman - to start praying and preparing for their marriage.

As I've often said, "the best place to launch the search for a life partner is from within you, not outside, not on social media, or dating websites. Start from within yourself."

You have to start by asking yourself…

- "Am I ready to get married?"

- "What and what should I start doing to prove that I'm ready?"

If you honestly ask yourself those questions, you'll discover several lifestyle changes that you must make. As you realize these changes and prayerfully begin to make them, your partner will manifest even before you say jack.

"It's an irony that some people want to marry a godly person, an honest person, a humble person, but they are godless, wayward, dishonest, proud and disrespectful. It doesn't work like that."

Like always begets like. So start the search for a life partner from yourself. Prayerfully discover and make changes to your attitudes. As you do, everything else begins to line up.

In this book, we want to encourage you to pray for your marriage, and let God take control. Even though prayer is often overlooked in the process of finding a spouse, it is one of the best things anyone can do to set things right.

Our prayer is that ***your marriage story will be a source of joy, a positive model for society, and not a negative example, in Jesus name***.

Pastor Daniel C. Okpara

Lesson 1: Who is a Godly Spouse?

By Doris

"There are two kinds of sparks, the one that goes off with a hitch like a match, but it burns quickly. The other is the kind that needs time, but when the flame strikes... it's eternal, don't forget that." - Anonymous

---

A Godly spouse is not someone who goes to church every day, sings in the choir, or even preaches from the pulpit.

A Godly spouse is not someone who prays in tongues or prophesies.

In fact, we advise anyone seeking a life partner not to be easily swayed into marriage by someone who puts on the face of **over spirituality** as they seek your hand in marriage. While spirituality is necessary, it is not a sign of Godliness.

"Many people can package themselves to look spiritual, while they are, in reality, fake."

Godliness is not marked by activity, or physical outlook. It is an attitude toward God, composed of the following essential elements:

- The fear of God

- The love of God

- The desire for God

- Hatred for evil

- Commitment to spiritual growth

- Testimony of salvation

- Membership to a local church

- Placement of God's Word above personal interests

1. The fear of God

Notice that I did not use the words, ***born again***. That phrase has been overly misunderstood because many who claim to be born again today are actually ***born against.*** They are everything wrong with the faith. So for now, let's stick with the ***fear of God***.

The Bible says:

If anyone respects and fears God, he will hate evil. For wisdom hates pride, arrogance, corruption, and deceit of every kind. - Proverbs 8:13 (TLB)

The fear of God is marked by a living conscience, remorse for wrongs, humility, hatred for evil and a lifestyle that strives to please God daily. It is an attitude that does not rejoice in evil, immorality, and sin; an attitude that recognizes that God will reward our actions of evil or good.

2. The Love of God

The love of God is manifested by

keeping the Words of God. Jesus said, "If you love me, keep my commandments. And I will pray the Father, and he shall give you the Comforter, that he may abide with you forever" (John 14:15-16).

One of the commandments of God emphasized throughout the scriptures is loving others and exercising forgiveness.

*He answered, "You shall love the Lord your God with all your heart and with all your soul and with all your strength and with all your mind, and your neighbor as yourself." - **Luke 10:27***

*Love must be sincere. Hate what is evil; cling to what is good **(Romans 12:9 -** NIV).*

Love does no harm to a neighbor.

*Therefore love is the fulfillment of the law (**Romans 13:10** - NIV).*

*If anyone says "I love God," but keeps on hating his brother, he is a liar; for if he doesn't love his brother who is right there in front of him, how can he love God whom he has never seen? (**1 John 4:20** - TLB)*

The Bible is saying that loving God is manifested by our relationship with others.

> *To be Godly therefore is to treat others the way we would want to be treated.*

A potential Godly spouse is therefore

one who is willing to respect others, forgive others, assist others as much as he or she can, and treat others fairly in business, and life.

3. The desire for God

The Psalmist said in Psalm 63:1, "O God, You are my God; I shall seek You earnestly; My soul thirsts for You, my flesh yearns for You, In a dry and weary land where there is no water."

The practice of godliness is an exercise or discipline that focuses on God; a heart that desires to walk with God. A Godly person aspires to please God in his or her way of life every day.

Godliness is not a state of being that you achieve, but a progressive, ongoing lifestyle of learning, leaning and depending on God.

4. Someone who hates evil

While a Godly person is not necessarily perfect - without errors and mistakes - he does not rejoice in iniquity.

When David was confronted with his sin, he fell face down, cried to God for mercy, and repented of his sins. That's the mark of Godliness - one always ready to repent of errors and sins when confronted with them.

5. Committed to spiritual growth

A potential Godly spouse should be one committed to spiritual growth. This will reflect in the person's most valued programs, events, and outings.

6. Someone with a testimony of salvation

There are many individuals in the church, but few with a testimony of salvation. Since Jesus is the first step to God, a potential Godly spouse must be someone who has accepted Christ as His LORD and personal Savior, and knows it. Not just a churchgoer.

As much as you can, ask questions like:

- "Are you going to heaven?"

- "When did you receive Christ as your LORD and personal savior?"

- "Can you share your salvation experience with me?"

While we warn us not to judge anyone, when it comes to someone you will be spending the rest of your life with, it's okay to learn as much as you can about the person's understanding and relationship with His maker.

7. Member of a local Church

If there's anything like being a registered member of a local church, then your potential Godly spouse should be one. He or she may not be sleeping in church, but the person should at least belong to a local church, fellowship, or prayer group, and have a good relationship with the leadership.

If you pick a wife or husband on the way, you may lose the person before you reach your destination. So ask questions like:

- "What church do you attend?"
- "Are you baptized in water?"

- "How is your relationship with your fellowship (church) leaders?"

All this may sound like you're hard on yourself. But you're only trying to do God's will.

8. Believes the Word of God above all

The word of God should be final, and the end of the discussion on any matter concerning a Christian. But where anyone can violate and set the word of God aside to pursue personal interests, that kind of person does not qualify as a godly spouse.

Lesson 2: How Do You *Find* A GODLY Spouse?

By Doris

"He who finds a wife finds what is good and receives favor from the LORD"

- Prov. 18:22

F*inding* a spouse is a serious business because not every woman will make a wife, and not every man will make a husband. There are many men, but few who can be husbands, and many women, but few who can be wives.

So, among the lot, you have to seek and find the one who will make your spouse.

Yes, there is a wife or husband out there. But you have to seek and find.

"A wife or husband is one who will share with you in your joy and pain for life."

We all want to get married to be happy, and that's great. But an essential requirement for a successful marriage is selflessness – putting the other person's welfare and happiness ahead of yours; doing everything you can to make the other person happy. Even though we may all claim to have that characteristic, it's not always the case (Proverbs 20:6). That's why prayer is necessary for guidance.

Marrying a Godly spouse should be every believer's desire. You cannot just marry anyone and then begin to pray for God to change the person. When Abraham wanted a wife for Isaac, he commanded his servant to ensure Isaac marries from among his people.

"He said to the senior servant in his household, the one in charge of all that he had, "Put your hand under my thigh.

"I want you to swear by the LORD, the God of heaven and the God of earth, that you will not get a wife for my son from the daughters of the Canaanites, among whom I am living

"But will go to my country and my own relatives and get a wife for my son

Isaac." (Gen. 24:1-4 AMP)

What was the problem with the people that was so repulsive to him to warrant an oath not get a wife from among them?

In Genesis 28:1, we see that Isaac also followed the same line of action:

So Isaac called for Jacob and blessed him. Then he commanded him: "Do not marry a Canaanite woman.

I'm sure the reason for this is because the ways of life of the Canaanites were quite different from that of Abraham and his family. No doubt, there were good women among the Canaanites, but it's better to marry from your fold than try to change someone into your way of life from scratch.

The book of 2 Corinthians 6:14 capture this more vividly:

"Don't be teamed with those who do not love the Lord, for what do the people of God have in common with the people of sin? How can light live with darkness? (TLB)

Desiring to marry a Godly person is the number one rule of Christian marriage. As I said, we must not fall into the temptation of saying that our faith will convert them. It's very risky to think that way.

With that said, let's now look at how to find a Godly spouse.

1. Set Realistic Expectations

Call it parameters, conditions, or expectations, it's the same thing. Set a realistic expectation of what you want in a spouse. I say realistic because, often times, our human expectations are vague, too carnal, and full of pride.

Everyone wants that tall, handsome, beautiful, easy-going, caring, jovial, well-to-do, humble, educated, supportive, churchy, well-traveled, fine-speaking, person. Unfortunately, these are wrong parameters for selecting a life partner. Those things are only found in movies and novels; and of course, celebrity marriages.

"The worse thing one can do to oneself is to model marriage after celebrities' relationships and marriages."

Realistic expectations are based on virtues and values, and not on physical appearances. Here are some of the conditions we always recommend that you consider in selecting who you want to marry:

a. Same faith: Not necessarily same denomination

b. Godliness: Based on what we discussed in the previous lesson

c. Vision and purpose: Can I relate to this person's life purpose. Where's this person going to? What's this person's direction and plan for life? Am I comfortable with that?

d. Life values and principles: What are the core values and beliefs this person is basing life on? What's this person's view about divorce, immorality, women, men, social media, lies, etc.? A person's core beliefs are their way of viewing and interpreting issues and subjects of life.

e. Teachability: Is this person a know-it-all kind of person? Does this person display a desire to learn and be taught?

A know-it-all kind of person is hazardous to marry

f. Closest friends: A person's closest friends are a clue of the kind of person you're dealing with. One may claim to be Godly and goodly, but watch for the friends. That's the kind of person they are.

g. Attitude to work: Manna does not fall from the sky. Money is not a result of miracles. So we highly advise against a person who believes that some miracles will happen and make him or her rich. We're not talking about how buoyant or not this person is, but the attitude this person has towards work.

h. Past Relationships: What happened to this person's past relationships, if any? How did it happen? If this person has divorced carelessly in the past, there's no guarantee it won't happen again.

i. Background: We, knowingly or unknowingly, reproduce 70-90% of what we learn from our parents or guardians. It's called modeling.

In as much as one can marry someone irrespective of the background as Christians, it is highly important that we consider the background. This will prepare us to pray very well, or know how to respond to certain issues when they manifest.

Another aspect of background consideration is to know the kind of relationship that exists between this person and the parents or guardians. A healthy relationship is a sign that this person will respect you and your parents as well, and vice versa.

As you can see, the above parameters have nothing to do with a person's physical looks. We believe that everyone is fearfully and wonderfully made. We are made in the image of God – all of us.

"If you marry someone based on looks, you'll have a hard time when the looks are not the same."

---

2. Trust Your Heart

I know you're asking, "So how will I know if this person is the right person or not?"

The answer is simple:

Trust your heart.

"Don't wait for a special dream, vision, or prophecy, to say this is the person. As you genuinely pray, somehow, you'll know this is the person or not."

Let me say that a Godly spouse does not fall from the sky. You may not have a dream or vision and hear God telling you, "Marry this person."

As a matter of fact, we advise against selecting a life partner based on dreams, because the human mind is a bit tricky at times. You may have some dream about a person, it doesn't mean you must marry this person. You must consider other factors as listed above.

It is also very wrong to pray prayers like, "God, if this person is your will for my life, then let so, and so things happen." That thing may happen, but does not mean God is the one behind it.

The place where you'll mostly know if this is the right person or not is in your heart. Somehow, as you pray, you'll have this peace and inner assurance that you're doing the right thing.

If, on the other hand, you have an inner withdrawal, a discomfort, some fears or restlessness, then you need to be careful and spend more time in prayers before making any serious commitment.

The most important decision you can make when seeking a life partner is not to be in haste. In fact, the Bible says that when we're in haste, we are not in faith (Isaiah 28:16b). Don't try to push things too quickly. A little more time can reveal some things that can save you plenty of issues later on.

Another thing you can do to help you out is to go for Godly counsel. Talk to someone older than you in age, experience, and spirituality; someone who will not pamper you, or try to give you a vision to prove his or her spirituality. This could be your pastor or anyone that is more spiritually mature.

The Bible says that "for lack of guidance, a nation falls. But with many counsels, you gain victory" (Proverbs 11:4).

"Don't fail for lack of counseling! Go for it. Marriage is a serious business."

Like I said, we warn people against

choosing who they will marry because someone gave them a prophecy or vision, or because they had some dreams. In as much as dreams, visions or other people's prophecies can provide us some clue; our choices should not be based on them.

Learn to trust your heart - not your head, not a dream and not a prophecy - for choosing who this person will be - after you have set Biblically based parameters. One thing is certain and sure - God will guide you.

Prayer: **To Let Go of Unrealistic Expectations**

"Heavenly Father, in the name of Jesus Christ, I ask that You protect my future spouse from any lies, tricks, traps or snares of the enemy. Keep them safe in all their ways and direct them to me.

O LORD, keep me from attaching myself to anyone out of desperation. Help me not to settle for a relationship that's second best, convenient, or one that feeds my insecurities. And when I meet my future spouse, please confirm to me that he/she is the one in ways I will be very sure.

It is written in James 1:5 that, "If any lacks wisdom, let him ask God, who

gives generously to all without reproach, and it will be given him."
LORD, I now ask You for wisdom and strength to let go of any luggage of past relationships, and prepare for the spouse You have chosen for me, in Jesus name.

LORD, help me to let go of any unrealistic expectations that will set me up for disappointment.

And let every stronghold of insecurity, habitual sins, selfishness, and emotionalism designed to yoke my life and bring an evil entanglement be broken this day, in Jesus name.

Lesson 3: Why Pray When Seeking a Life Partner?

By Daniel

"When you fish for love, bait with your heart, not your brain."

\- Mark Twain

Ecclesiastes 3: 1 says that *"There is a time for everything and a season for every activity under heaven."* There is a time to seek a wife or a husband. There is a time to get married. There is a time to quit *'single life'* and embark on the marriage journey.

Marriage is an exciting adventure.

Unfortunately, many have made a shipwreck of it. The number of divorce cases keeps increasing despite the number of books and marriage counseling out there. Why?

I believe that one of the primary reasons for the increasing number of failed marriages is because people want to run marriage with their ideas alone, and not that of God, who made marriage. Many believe that since marriage is more physical than spiritual, God is not a factor in the equation. Unfortunately, it's not working.

> *"Marriage is one area where*
> *the wisdom of man has failed*
> *woefully."*

God is the person who gave out the first

bride, Eve. He is the one who instituted the covenant of marriage. He is interested in the success of the institution He set up.

If we're going to get the best out of our marriages and relationships, then we must recognize the source of marriage, and as much as we can, make efforts to run our marriages using the owner's manual for it.

I drive a Honda car for example. It will be unfair for me to run the vehicle using Toyota manual and parts. No matter how safe and economical the Toyota parts are, I'll be doing myself lots of disservices to drive my Honda car with Toyota parts.

So, if you feel you've come to the stage of

your life – to seek a life partner –one of the best things you can do is to pray.

"Prayer is one of the most powerful ways to start your marriage journey. It will take the unforeseen circumstances off your chest and keep them at God's feet. It will prepare the way for you and make the crooked places straight."

What will prayer do for you as you seek a life partner?

There are so many great things prayer will achieve for you; but first, let me tell you what prayer will not do.

First, praying for a life partner does not mean you'll get a perfect person. Far from it. No matter how godly we are, we are all working towards perfection. No one is perfect yet, as long as we are still on earth.

Secondly, prayer is not intended to convince God to send you that handsome, beautiful, young, tall, spotless, caring, educated, out-going, prayerful, wealthy, and magnanimous angel. As much as these qualities are great, they are our mental creations motivated by movies and not the basis for praying for a life partner.

Thirdly, prayer is not designed to be a means of changing someone from an unbeliever to a believer. We've met with many young people who think that when they marry someone, they will change that person; or that as they pray, someone will eventually change and become the kind of person they want. From our experience, this has not always come out well.

Yes, prayer does change people. But it should not be used as a bargain to get God to change someone that you have decided to marry against Biblical counsel and input from those older than you.

Fourthly, praying for a life partner (and ultimately for your marriage) does not mean you will not have issues in your marriage. Not at all. Praying for a godly spouse does not exempt one from the challenges of marriage. However, it will position you for victory, from time to time. Issues will always come up, but God will always give you wisdom for victory. Somehow, you will always win.

So what will prayer do for you in marriage?

First, prayer changes you. You will begin to see things differently from the way you used to see them. It will soften your heart, make you more humble, take away haste and anxiety from you, and make you calm.

Secondly, prayer helps you discern between wolves and sheep. The Bible says that everyone claims to be faithful, but it's tough to find one who is truly faithful.

You'll meet with so many people interested in having a relationship with you. Usually, they will come in the name of having your interest at heart. If you're not careful, you'll surrender your defenses because of their promises.

But as you pray, somehow, your heart will begin to discern between the lines. Events will start to unfold to give you an insight about who you're dealing with, and you'll know whether to draw the line or proceed.

Thirdly, prayer will position you at the right place. Success in life is all about positioning. There's a place to be, and when to be at this location, to meet with your spouse to be. As you sincerely and intentionally pray, activities will begin to line up to bring you to relevant places that will usher you into your breakthrough.

Fourthly, prayer will destroy spiritual

barriers and obstacles that cause marital delays. It will help you reject curses, shatter demonic and witchcraft manipulations that work against marriage plans and homes.

Yes, there are issues that are beyond the physical that can try to scuttle your marriage, lead you astray or cause you heartbreak. But as you pray, the power of God will begin to move in the spirit to destroy these spiritual barriers and manifest your desires and breakthrough.

Finally, prayer will give you the wisdom to prepare, and help you in the selection process. Somehow, it will cause things to work out in ways you least expected. It will give you a sense of inner assurance that God is in control.

"When we intentionally pray for our marriages, great things happen. Great changes take place, beginning from the inside of us. Life-threatening mistakes are avoided and great blessings manifest."

I believe that my earnest prayers played a vital role in the choice of the person that I married, especially when I consider the circumstances that brought us together.

I had already paid a visit to the family of someone else I wanted to marry. The family had welcomed me heartily and was waiting for me to start the marriage process. On the other side, someone else had also visited the family of my wife today, and they were making plans to commence the marriage process. But somehow, we met, and everything changed.

Somehow, we knew we were made for each other. As we tried hard not to make it work, because of the other commitment, it just continued, and then worked beyond our expectations. Today, I look back and I'm happy I prayed for God's help while seeking a life partner.

I'm not saying we don't have issues. We do. But all said and done, we are getting better and growing stronger together.

We encourage you to pray earnestly as you desire and seek a life partner, because as the Bible says, "It is not of him that willeth, neither him that runneth, but God that showeth mercy" (Romans 9:16). "The horse is ready for battle, but victory belongs to God" (Proverbs 21:31).

Lesson 4: How to Prepare For Marriage

By Doris

P reparation is the key to success in everything we do in life. It is your level of readiness that determines how far you will go in whatever you pursue.

People marry for different reasons. Some marry for money, some for sex, some out of sympathy, some out of loneliness, some for compensation, and so on. Whatever the reason you want to get married, be sure you're not being rushed into it - either by yourself or by someone else. You should be sure you are ready and prepared for it.

We've seen a couple of cases where someone says, "I wasn't really ready for this. I don't know what happened. I just know that I'm not ready for this yet."

Can you imagine that?

Before you get married, be sure you are ready – both mentally and physically.

How?

1. Define Your Purpose for Marriage

To be on the right path, you must come to terms with why you really want to get married. Are you looking for someone to pay your bills? Are you looking for a sex partner? Are you looking for someone to get the shame of not being married out of you?

Why do you want to get married?

We recommend that your reason for getting married should be based on the fact that you've seen the need for a companion. You've come to the point in your life where you believe that you need someone to share your life, visions, ideas, challenges, prayers, and plans with.

2. Get Busy With Your Life

Did you notice that before God gave Adam a wife, he was very busy with his work?

God said, "It's not good for the Man to be alone; I'll make him a helper, a companion." So God formed from the dirt of the ground all the animals of the field and all the birds of the air. He brought them to the Man to see what he would name them.

Whatever the Man called each living creature, that was its name. The Man named the cattle, named the birds of the air, named the wild animals; but he didn't find a suitable companion. Genesis 2:18-20 (MSG)

If you thought that naming all the animals in the world was an easy thing, then you need to think again. Adam was so busy with His assignment that God said, "No, this guy needs someone to help him."

---

*"Marriage is not to be
seen as a means of
escaping from single life,
but a means of fulfilling
God's assignment for
your life."*

Mandy Hale, the author of the book, Beautiful Uncertainty, said, "Hope for love, pray for love, wish for love, dream for love...but don't put your life on hold waiting for love."

She's right.

Get busy with your work. Have a life, whether you're a man or woman. Don't just stay at home waiting to get married. Advance your studies, learn some skills, start a business. Whatever that can add value to your life, get busy with it. In your **busyness**, your spouse will be revealed.

3. Be Willing to Take Responsibility

Marriage is all about responsibility. Bills will increase. Offences will increase. So, are you ready to face challenges and overcome them without blaming anyone? Are you ready to get out there and work very hard to support your spouse? Are you willing to forget about your happiness and work for the happiness of someone else?

Are you ready?

That's basically what marriage is all about...

Responsibility.

> *That is why a man leaves his father and mother and is united to his wife, and they become one flesh. (Gen 2:24)*

Leaving father and mother here doesn't mean to disown your parents or stop caring for them. It means to create your own life; to face your own challenges, take your own decisions without parental influence, and fight and win your battles.

4. Get Ready to Lose Your Freedom

As a single person, you're free to do so many things. But once you're married, you'll lose that freedom. You'll be subject to someone's interference in your choice of words, a place to live, jobs to take, etc. So in a way, you'll lose some freedom. And you'll have to do it with joy.

So think about it for a while.

5. Get Ready to Accept Your Bible Role

Marital roles are clearly defined in scripture. Husbands have roles to play, and wives have roles to play. The man is to love the wife as Christ loved the Church and was willing to die for her. It was after Christ died for the Church that he became her head. The woman also must be prepared to submit to and obey her husband.

You wives must submit to your husbands' leadership in the same way you submit to the Lord.

For a husband is in charge of his wife in the same way Christ is in charge of his body the Church. (He gave his very life to take care of it and be its Savior!)

So you wives must willingly obey your husbands in everything, just as the Church obeys Christ.

And you husbands, show the same kind of love to your wives as Christ showed to the Church when he died for her, to make her holy and clean, washed by baptism and God's Word; so that he could give her to himself as a glorious Church without a single spot or wrinkle or any other blemish, being holy and without a single fault.

That is how husbands should treat their wives, loving them as parts of themselves. For since a man and his wife are now one, a man is really doing himself a favor and loving himself when he loves his wife!

No one hates his own body but lovingly cares for it, just as Christ cares for his body the Church, of which we are parts. – Ephesians 5:22-30 (TLB)

Read this scripture again and again. That's the summary of the roles of a Godly couple. Are you ready to accept that?

Lesson 5: How to Pray For a Godly Spouse

By Daniel

Trust in the Lord with all thine heart; and lean not unto thine own understanding. In all thy ways acknowledge him, and he shall direct thy paths.

Be not wise in thine own eyes: fear the Lord, and depart from evil. It shall be health to thy navel, and marrow to thy bones. - Prov. 3:5-8

If you forget everything, don't forget this: *Marriage is God's plan, not yours.*

When we genuinely pray for our marriages, what we are doing is saying:

"LORD, I understand that marriage is Your making. I confess that I cannot be successful in it by my ideas. Help me in the journey."

"When we pray, we are trusting God and acknowledging Him to direct us. We recognize that we can of our selves do nothing. We need God's help."

Here's the thing. If you start praying for your marriage, your perceptions and understanding of marriage will drastically improve.

You'll begin to realize that many things you read on social media and dating websites about marriage are not the accurate representation of marriage. You'll be amazed how your ***"this-is-what-I-want-and-how-I-want-it-to-be"*** approach will be adjusted to God's will.

Simply put, you'll be changed inside out.

Prayer is the best way to turn your marriage over to God and make Him the pilot of the journey. And when He is in control, we can be sure that we'll be safe no matter what happens.

He says:

"When you go through deep waters and great trouble, I will be with you. When you go through rivers of difficulty, you will not drown! When you walk through the fire of oppression, you will not be burned up—the flames will not consume you." - Isaiah 43:2

In essence, when you come to times of confusion and heat, because God is with you, you will be delivered. Somehow, you'll find a way.

Getting Started

There are over 50 prayer points in this book arranged under different headings. Choose a prayer heading and go over it per day. When you're done, come back and start afresh.

Praying to find a spouse is not a one-day thing. That means you don't just pray today and that's it. You need to spend many days, even weeks or months as you pray.

From time to time, add fasting to your prayers.

And don't forget that the most important thing you need as you pray for a spouse is peace.

You will not have direction when your mind is in turmoil. As much as possible, you must let God take away your anxiety and restlessness to get married. The

Bible says that as we pray in line with God's will, that God hears and answers us.

"You need to believe that God is working out things for your good. He is sending the right person your way, and you'll know it when you see the person."

Be anxious for nothing, but in everything by prayer and supplication, with thanksgiving, let your requests be made known to God; and the peace of God, which surpasses all understanding, will guard your hearts and minds through Christ Jesus (Philipians 4:6-7).

Prayer 1: **Preparation of the Heart**

"Keep your heart with all diligence; for out of it are the issues of life." – Prov 4:23

The Living Bible puts that passage this way: *"Above all else, guard your affections. For they influence everything else in your life."*

Your heart condition is the primary key in your quest to find a spouse. You need to ask God to sanctify your heart and deliver you from all kinds of negative emotions, false motives, and anxieties.

Read and Meditate

- Philippians 4:6-7

- Matthew 6:25-34

Prayer Points

1. Thank God because He has a good plan towards you, to give you an expected end (Jeremiah 29:11)

2. Thank God for the gift of life

3. Read Isaiah 34:16 and thank God for your spouse. God has given a decree, and you will not lack your mate

4. Thank God because He alone is the One who gives good and perfect gifts (James 1:17)

5. Thank God because before the foundation of this world He has someone for you (Jeremiah 1:5)

6. Thank God because He is working behind the scenes to bring your right partner to you

7. Ask God to forgive you in any way you have demonstrated fear, doubt, and unbelief regarding your marriage and life partner.

8. Ask God to take away from you all forms of anxiety and worry about getting married.

9. Ask God for peace of mind and to help you maintain calmness regarding marriage henceforth.

10. Read 2 Timothy 1:7 and bind the spirit of fear from your life

11. Receive the spirit of love, power and sound mind, in Jesus name

Prayer 2: **The Power of Patience**

"But they that wait upon the Lord shall renew their strength; they shall mount up with wings as eagles; they shall run, and not be weary, and they shall walk, and not faint." – Isa. 40:31

When we pray, we need patience to receive the promises.

Patience is the ability to remain in joy until the answers manifest. It is the grace to stay in God and not wander off until God sends your expectation.

---

*"As humans, we calculate things based on our timeframes. Sometimes, we look at things and say, **"God, I'm out of time."** But, that's not true. You're not out of time, and God is right on time in your life."*

Today, you're going to pray for grace to remain in joy, while waiting for the manifestation of your spouse.

Read and Meditate

- Proverbs 14:29
- 1 Corinthians 13:4-5
- Ephesians 4:2
- Romans 12:12
- Galatians 6:9

- Psalm 37:7
- Colossians 3:12

Prayer Points

1. Thank God for the Gift of the Holy Spirit, who can make you patient and joyful in waiting.

2. Ask God to baptize you with a calmness spirit.

3. Ask God to take away from you any form of restlessness and anxiety about marriage.

4. Declare and say, "O LORD, from today onwards, I refuse to fret up and down, on account of a life partner, in Jesus name."

5. Ask God to uproot haste, envy and quick temper from your life, in Jesus name.

6. Ask God for the wisdom to unconditionally celebrate with others as they are getting their blessings, and not to compare yourself with them, in Jesus name

7. Ask God to grace you with love, tolerance, and humility.

8. Ask God to baptize you with joy as you wait for the appearing and manifestation of your spouse.

9. Ask God to empower you to continue to do good to others, for in due season, you will reap if you faint not.

10. Declare and say, "LORD, I refuse to faint from doing good. Make me a pillar of comfort and support for others, in Jesus name."

Prayer 3: Cleansing from Negative Family History

W e're all coming from a family. Whether we like it or not, our family history has a role it is playing in our present life. When we get born again, we receive power to prayerfully disconnect ourselves from every negative family inheritance and claim the positive ones.

For example, if you're coming from a polygamous home, or a home where parents usually fought or even divorced, remarried, or where adultery was always happening, or poverty was a threat – then you need to pray and renounce all forms of covenants, curses and negative traits that such would have left for the children of the family.

I have written a couple of books on breaking curses, where I spent more time dealing with the issue of *family line and generational curses*. You may want to get those books if you need more information on this.

In this book, I'll only lead you with prayers to completely disconnect and renounce all forms of spiritual barriers against your life coming from your family line or history.

Read and Meditate

Galatians 3:13 - Christ hath redeemed us from the curse of the law, being made a curse for us: for it is written, Cursed is every one that hangeth on a tree.

Ezekiel 18:20 - The soul that sinneth, it shall die. The son shall not bear the iniquity of the father, neither shall the father bear the iniquity of the son: the righteousness of the righteous shall be upon him, and the wickedness of the wicked shall be upon him.

Recommendation

Pray these prayers in the midnight hours – anything between 12:00 am – 4:00 am. And pray these prayers with authority. You may also need to pray these prayers more than once.

Prayer

1. Heavenly Father, I thank You once again for the marriage institution. I thank You because my marriage will work, in Jesus name. (Psalm 127:1-2).

2. LORD, I ask You to show me mercy as I take steps towards my marriage henceforth. May I not be a victim of my family errors, sins, and destruction, in Jesus name. (Rom 9:15-16)

3. LORD, I ask for forgiveness from all forms of negative generational covenants, false ways and sins *(name them, e.g. adultery, fights, spiritism, idolatry, etc.)* that have placed different kinds of spiritual limitations on the family members. Please LORD, let Your mercy prevail over my family henceforth, in Jesus name.

4. LORD, I know that these sins have opened doors for demons to operate in the family. But right now LORD, by the Blood of Jesus Christ, I receive forgiveness for my family and at this

moment, close all the doors through which demons are operating against my family and me, in Jesus name

5. I plead the Blood of Jesus Christ over my life and my family generations, in Jesus name.

6. LORD, I bind any demon operating against my life and family as a result of past parental sins. I command these demons to leave my life and family right now and go back to the abyss, in Jesus name.

7. I command any spiritual stronghold or negative characteristic inherited from my past lifestyle or my family line to be destroyed right now, in Jesus name.

8. Every spirit of confusion, delay, poverty, fear, affliction, marital crisis,

that has entered my family line and has been working against my life and family, I bind you and cast you all into the abyss in Jesus name.

9. I overthrow every stronghold of the enemy in my life and family today. I command every wicked strong man or woman enforcing evil agreements and decisions from my family generations against my life, receive fire and pack out of my family to the abyss, in Jesus name.

10. Today, O LORD, I break every yoke of inherited marital delay and disappointment in marriage, in Jesus name.

11. This day, LORD, I decree total healing and restoration from any form of affliction in my life and family,

coming from my family generation, in Jesus name.

12. Every generational curse and covenant that will stand against my marriage be broken by fire, in Jesus name.

13. I renounce every demonic marital covenant in my life and family, in Jesus name.

14. Every vow, promise, oath or covenant that is designed to hinder and obstruct my marriage, I renounce you all this moment, in the name of Jesus Christ.

15. I renounce and bind every spirit of polygamy, divorce, immorality and adultery. I cast these spirits out of my family, generation and send them back

to the abyss. I decree that these sins will not manifest again in my life and family, in Jesus name.

16. LORD, I release my spouse from any witchcraft coven and satanic bondage right now, in Jesus name

17. I command my spouse to be set free from any form of generational curse or covenant blinding and hindering ...from locating me, in Jesus name.

18. Today, O LORD, I decree that my marriage will be a blessing to this generation, in Jesus name.

19. Heavenly Father, baptize me with wisdom to run my marriage, relate with my spouse and manage my home. May I not repeat the sins of the past, in Jesus name.

20. Father in Heaven, fill my home and coming marriage with the peace that passes understanding and exemplifies Biblical marriage, in Jesus name.

Prayer 4: **For Direction and Guidance**

"I will instruct you (says the Lord) and guide you along the best pathway for your life; I will advise you and watch your progress. 9 Don't be like a senseless horse or mule that has to have a bit in its mouth to keep it in line!"

- Psalm 32:8-9

The most important thing you need as you seek a life partner is wisdom and clear direction to make the right choice and stick with it.

No, God won't write the person's name in the sky, or tattoo it on your forehead, or shout it to you in the dream. But as you pray, and the time is right, He'll open doors...after He closes a few others first. He'll bring discussions, information, and opportunities your way. He'll give you the inner witness in your heart that He confirms in other ways.

His methods are unlimited, but one thing is sure: He will guide you.

Read and Meditate

- Isaiah 30:21

- Psalm 32:8-9

- Psalm 23

- Proverbs 16:9

Prayer

1. Dear Heavenly Father, I trust You

with all my heart, I don't want to rely on my own understanding. I commit myself to acknowledging You in all my ways, and I'm trusting You to make my paths straight as I expect a life partner, in Jesus name. (Proverbs 3:5-6).

2. LORD, I claim Your promise to instruct me, and to teach me in the way I should go, and to counsel me with Your eye upon me. Thank You for Your promise of guidance, in Jesus name (Psalm 32:8).

3. My Father in Heaven, You do know that all my ways seem so right in my eyes. That's right LORD. Most times I'm hard headed and do things my own way. I have trouble seeing my own errors. Please, LORD, I surrender to You this day and ask You to purge my motive of

all forms of carnality, and fill my mind with Your Holy thoughts, even as I seek for a life partner, in Jesus name. (Proverbs 16:2)

4. Dear LORD Jesus Christ, in this matter of a life partner, I pray as You prayed while on earth: "I seek not My own will but the will of Him who sent me." LORD, I want what You want for me, and I trust You to reveal that to me, as I wait on Thee, in Jesus name. (John 5:30)

5. LORD, "Let me hear Your lovingkindness in the morning; For I trust in You; Teach me the way in which I should walk; For to You I lift up my soul" in Jesus name.(Psalm 143:8).

6. LORD, You said, If I ask, that I'll

receive, if I seek, I'll find, and if I knock, the door will be opened for me. I am now asking You for guidance, seeking Your will, and knocking on Your door of heaven. LORD, cause me to receive, find and let the door be opened for me, in Jesus name. (Matthew 7:7-8)

7. LORD, You said You will teach the humble in Your way and lead them to what is right. I am asking You once again for the spirit of humility. Teach me in your way and lead me in the path which is right, in Jesus name. Proverbs 25:9)

8. LORD, You're the God of my salvation. Make me know Your ways, O LORD; Teach me Your paths, and lead me in Your truth; For You I wait all the day, in Jesus name. (Psalm 25:4-5).

9. O LORD, please reveal my spouse to me. Order my steps to meet the person You have ordained for me, and whenever I see the person, LORD, empower me to recognize it, in Jesus name.

10. Father LORD, help me to stick with Your timing and not rush into marriage out of pressure, frustration or desperation, in Jesus name.

11. O LORD, give me wisdom and discernment to recognize my spouse, in Jesus name.

12. I frustrate every power that will hinder or stop me from recognizing and marrying my God ordained spouse, in Jesus name.

13. Every manipulative and deceptive

spirit projected against me in marriage, I come against you this day. I bind you all and cast you into the abyss in Jesus name.

14. O LORD, expose every hidden thing that will enable me to make the right choice in my relationship, in Jesus name.

15. My marriage will surely glorify God, in Jesus name.

Prayer 5: **Prayer of Confirmation**

---

1. Bind every spirit of error in marriage.

2. Pray that past mistakes will not stand against you.

3. Command the spirit of fear and doubt to leave

4. Bind every spirit of pride and inferiority complex in your life.

5. Pray for peace in your heart when you find your spouse.

6. Pray that you will not fall into the hand of deceivers and wicked counselors.

7. Pray for clarity of direction

concerning your spouse

8. Pray that God will use godly men and women to confirm your spouse

Prayer 6: **Break Spiritual Barriers**

1. Bind demonic watchers and spirits assigned to monitor the process of your marriage.

2. Come against every power of near miracle situation.

3. Break every yoke of failure and premature death in marriage.

4. Come against every spirit of adversity in marriage.

5. Come against every arranged disaster during your marriage.

6. Come against satanic arrows before, during and after marriage.

7. Pray that your marriage will command the favors and blessings of God.

8. Pray that your marriage will open new doors of prosperity and favors for you.

9. Pray that your marriage will not inherit evil from either family.

10. Pray that your businesses, job or ministry will not downsize after marriage.

11. Pray that your marriage will be a success story.

12. Thank God for seeing you through the whole process of marriage.

13. Pray that your potential in-laws will be a blessing to you, in Jesus name.

14. Pray that money will be readily provided for your marriage.

15. Pray that the process of your marriage will be safe and peaceful.

16. Commit your spouse to God in prayer that God will clothe them with fire throughout the process of the marriage.

17. Pray that his presence will go with you all the way.

18. Give Him thanks and praise for everything in advance.

God

Bless

You

Get in Touch

We love testimonies. We love to hear what God is doing around the world as people draw close to Him in prayer. Please share your story with us.

Also, please consider giving this book a review on Amazon and checking out our other titles at www.amazon.com/author/danielokpara .

I also invite you to check out our website at www.BetterLifeWorld.org and consider joining our newsletter, which we send out once in a while with great tips, testimonies, and revelations from God's Word for victorious living.

Feel free to drop us your prayer request. We will join faith with you, and God's power will be released in your life and the issue in question.

About The Author

Daniel Chika Okpara is a husband, father, pastor, businessman and lecturer. He has authored over 50 life transforming books on business, prayer, relationship and victorious living.

He is the president of Better Life World Outreach Centre -www.betterlifeworld.org - a non-denominational evangelism ministry committed to global prayer revival and evangelism.

He is a Computer Engineer by training, and holds a Master's Degree in Theology from Cornerstone Christian University. He is married to Prophetess Doris Okpara, his prayer warrior, best friend and biggest support in life. They are blessed with two lovely children.

Other Books by the Same Author

1. Prayer Retreat: 21 Days Devotional With Over 500 Prayers & Declarations to Destroy Stubborn Demonic Problems.

2. HEALING PRAYERS & CONFESSIONS

3. 200 Violent Prayers for Deliverance, Healing, and Financial Breakthrough.

4. Hearing God's Voice in Painful Moments

5. Healing Prayers: Prophetic Prayers that Brings Healing

6. Healing WORDS: Daily Confessions & Declarations to Activate Your Healing.

7. Prayers That Break Curses and Spells and Release Favors and Breakthroughs.

8. 120 Powerful Night Prayers That Will

Change Your Life Forever.

9. How to Pray for Your Children Everyday

10. How to Pray for Your Family

11. Daily Prayer Guide

12. Make Him Respect You: 31 Very Important Relationship Advice for Women to Make their Men Respect them.

13. How to Cast Out Demons from Your Home, Office & Property

14. Praying Through the Book of Psalms

15. The Students' Prayer Book

16. How to Pray and Receive Financial Miracle

17. Powerful Prayers to Destroy Witchcraft Attacks.

18. Deliverance from Marine Spirits

19. Deliverance From Python Spirit

20. Anger Management God's Way

NOTES

Printed in Great Britain
by Amazon